SCHOLASTIC

English Practice for

Year 4

Ages 8-9

Year 4

This book belongs to:

....

English Year 4, Book 1

Book End, Range Road, Witney, Oxfordshire, OX29 0YD

www.scholastic.co.uk

© 2014, Scholastic Ltd

1 2 3 4 5 6 7 8 9   4 5 6 7 8 9 0 1 2 3

British Library Cataloguing-in-Publication Data
A catalogue record for this book is available from the British Library.

ISBN 978-1407-14199-2
Printed and bound in China by Hung Hing Offset Printing

Due to the nature of the web we cannot guarantee the content or links of any site mentioned. We strongly recommend that teachers check websites before using them in the classroom.

Editorial
Rachel Morgan, Melissa Somers, Sarah Sodhi, Catherine Baker and Fiona Tomlinson

Design
Scholastic Design Team: Neil Salt, Nicolle Thomas and Oxford Designers & Illustrators Ltd

Cover Design
Neil Salt

Illustration
Aleksander Sotirovski (Beehive Illustration)

Acknowledgements
The publishers gratefully acknowledge permission to reproduce the following copyright material: **David Higham Associates** for permission to use the poem 'Cats' from *The Children's Bells* by Eleanor Farjeon. Poem © 1957, Eleanor Farjeon (1957, Oxford University Press). **Hachette Children's Books** for permission to use an extract from *Earth Watch: Water for all* by Bender Richardson White. Text © 2000, Bender Richardson White (2000, Franklin Watts). Every effort has been made to trace copyright holders for the works reproduced in this book, and the publishers apologise for any inadvertent omissions.

Contents

Why buy this book?

This series has been designed to support the introduction of the new National Curriculum in schools in England. The new curriculum is more challenging in English and includes the requirement for children's understanding to be secure before moving on. These practice books will help your child practise all of the skills they will learn at school, including some topics they might not have encountered previously.

How to use this book

- The content is divided into National Curriculum topics (for example, Spelling, Grammar, Comprehension and so on). Find out what your child is doing in school and dip into the relative practice activities as required.

- Let your child know you are sharing the activities and support if necessary using the helpful quick tips at the top of most pages.

- Keep the working time short and come back to an activity if your child finds it too difficult. Ask your child to note any areas of difficulty. Don't worry if your child does not 'get' a concept first time, as children learn at different rates and content is likely to be covered throughout the school year.

- Check your child's answers using the answers section at the end of this book.

- Give lots of encouragement and tick off the progress chart as your child completes each chapter.

How to use the book

This tells you which topic you're working on.

This is the title of the activity.

Letters in slashes (like this) tell you it's the sound and not the spelling.

These boxes will help you with the activity.

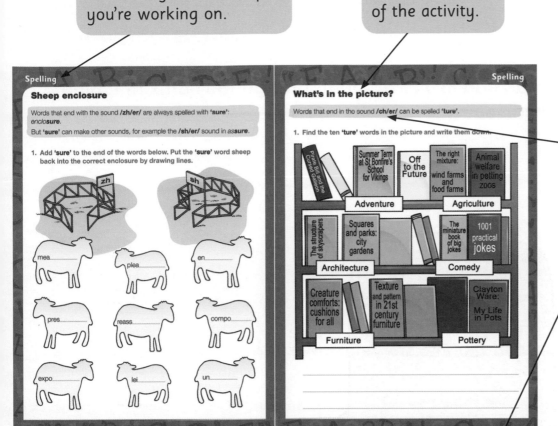

This is the instruction text. It tells you what to do.

Follow the instruction to complete the activity.

You might have to write on lines, in boxes, draw or circle things.

If you need help, ask an adult!

Words ending in 'l'

Remember – in words like *hop* and *control*, you double the final consonant before adding a suffix.

1. **All of these words end in 'l'. Put them through the suffix machine and write new correct words.**

peel

marvel

peril

control

novel

final

travel

propel

signal

jewel

football

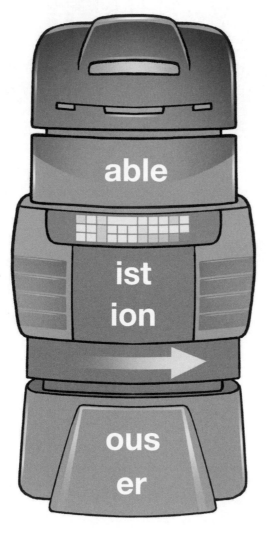

able

ist
ion

ous
er

_____

_____

_____

_____

_____

_____

_____

_____

_____

_____

_____

'i' or 'y'?

In some words the long vowel **/igh/** sound is spelled with a **'y'**: *spy*, *by*, *my*.
BUT in some words the short vowel **/i/** sound can also be spelled with a **'y'**,
such as *gym*.

1. **The words below are not spelled correctly. Correct them by changing the 'i' to a 'y'.**

histerical

simptom

lirics

simmetry

simpathy

cristal

sistem

mistery

tipical

cignet

Encourage the 'ou'

Sometimes the letters **'ou'** make the sound **/u/**.

1. Complete each sentence by adding an 'ou' word from the box.

> touch   young   country   double   cousin
> couple   flourish   tough   encourage

a. Don't _____ the statue or it will fall over.

b. The _____ man ran the marathon.

c. I went to live in another _____.

d. There is a _____ of apples in the bowl.

e. The teacher said he would _____

our homework because we were not listening.

f. My _____ lives in New York.

g. Your cactus will occasionally need water if you want

it to _____.

h. It was a _____ climb but we made it!

i. I think I will _____ my friend to

enter the auditions.

Irregular and illogical

When you add the prefixes **'ir'** and **'il'** to words, you change their meaning.

- **'il'** and **'ir'** mean *not.*

1. Find the meaning of these words using a dictionary.

> legal   logical   regular   resistible   reversible   rational

2. Add **'il'** or **'ir'** to each word from question 1 to create correct new words. Use each one in a sentence of your own.

a. _____

_____

b. _____

_____

c. _____

_____

d. _____

_____

e. _____

_____

f. _____

_____

Spelling

'in' or 'im'?

Here are two more prefixes which change a word from one meaning into its opposite.

● **'in'** and **'im'** mean *not*.

1. Add 'im' or 'in' to these words to make their opposites.

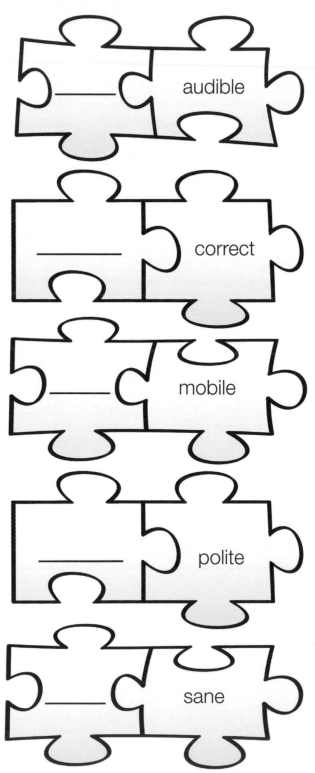

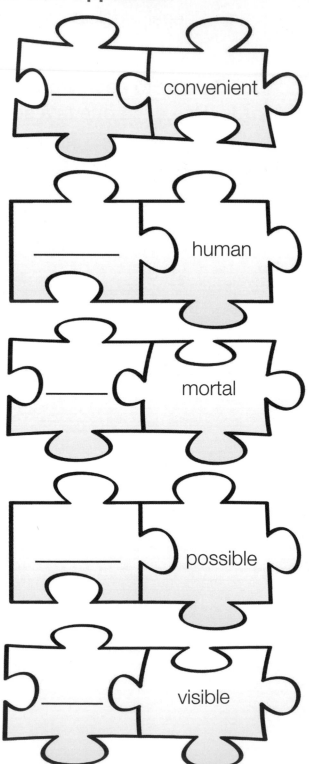

_____ audible

_____ convenient

_____ correct

_____ human

_____ mobile

_____ mortal

_____ polite

_____ possible

_____ sane

_____ visible

Muddled words

- The prefix **'re'** means *again* or *back*.
- The prefix **'inter'** means *between* or *among*.

1. Add the correct prefix and write the words in the boxes.

lude   fresh   related   appear   decorate
treat   continental   arrange   face   mingle

re

inter

Super sub prefix machine

- **'sub'** means *under* or *below*.
- **'super'** means *above*, *over* or *beyond*.

1. Add 'super' or 'sub' to these words to make new real words.

category _____

standard _____

computer _____

editor _____

sonic _____

impose _____

merge _____

power _____

2. Create some new words by adding 'sub' or 'super' to words you know.

_____ _____

_____ _____

_____ _____

_____ _____

Adding 'ation'

Adding **'ation'** to a verb changes it into a noun.

- Most words just add **'ation'**: *inform – information*
- If the words ends in **'e'**, take off the **'e'** before adding **'ation'**: *sense – sensation*
- If the word ends in **'ate'**, take off the **'ate'** before adding **'ation'**: *accelerate – acceleration*
- If the words ends in **'y'**, change the **'y'** to **'ic'** before adding **'ation'**: *classify – classification*

1. Add 'ation' to the words below following the rules above.

admire _____

relocate _____

justify _____

translate _____

animate _____

educate _____

observe _____

accommodate _____

anticipate _____

identify _____

Adjective to adverb

If the adjective ends in **'y'**, change the **'y'** to **'i'**, then add the **'ly'**.
hungry – hungrily

1. **Change the adjectives in the first column into adverbs. The first one has been done for you.**

Adjective	Adverb
angry	angrily
anxious	
bad	
careful	
clumsy	
correct	
greedy	
happy	
hungry	
immediate	
quiet	
serious	

Adding 'ly' to words ending in 'le'

If the adjective ends in consonant + **'le'**, remove **'le'** and add **'ly'**.

If the adjective ends in vowel + **'le'**, just add **'ly'**.

For example: *simple – simply* but *sole – solely*.

1. **Change these adjectives into adverbs following the rule.**

Adjective	Adverb
incredible	_____
hostile	_____
probable	_____
agile	_____
terrible	_____

2. **Use the words you created in question 1 to complete these sentences.**

"Well, I think we're _____ looking at a world record, Jeff."

"Sure, Matt. The boy's _____ talented."

"He moves so _____ – on this apparatus, there's no knowing what he's capable of."

"And now he's fallen! The crowd are reacting quite _____ about that."

"What a _____ embarrassing moment for team GB."

Sheep enclosure

Words that end with the sound **/zh/er/** are always spelled with **'sure'**: *enclo**sure***.

But **'sure'** can make other sounds, for example the **/sh/er/** sound in *as**sure***.

1. **Add 'sure' to the end of the words below. Put the 'sure' word sheep back into the correct enclosure by drawing lines.**

zh

sh

mea_____

plea_____

en_____

pres_____

reass_____

compo_____

expo_____

lei_____

un_____

What's in the picture?

Words that end in the sound **/ch/er/** can be spelled **'ture'**.

1. **Find the ten 'ture' words in the picture and write them down.**

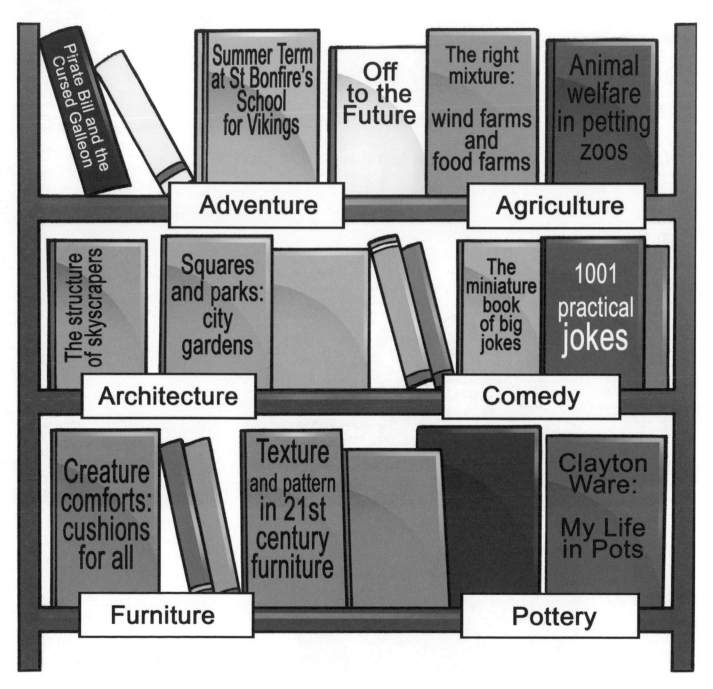

_____

_____

_____

How to add 'ous'

Adding **'ous'** to a verb or a noun makes an adjective.

- Most words just add **'ous'**: *poison – poisonous*
- Words ending in **'e'**, take off the **'e'** before adding **'ous'**: *fame – famous*
- Words ending in **'y'**, take off the **'y'** and add **'i'** before adding **'ous'**: *vary – various*
- Keep the **'e'** if the word ends with a **/j/** sound before adding **'ous'**: *outrage – outrageous*

1. Use the rules above to add 'ous' to these words.

courage _____

harmony _____

envy _____

poison _____

glory _____

fame _____

vary _____

adventure _____

ous

luxury _____

outrage _____

'tion', 'sion', 'ssion', 'cian' assembly line

Words which end with the sound **/sh/u/n/** can be spelled in four different
ways: **'tion'**, **'sion'**, **'ssion'** or **'cian'**.
Remember:

- To add **'tion'** take off the **'t'** or **'te'** first.
- To add **'sion'** take off the **'d'**, **'se'** or **'de'** first.
- To add **'ssion'** take off the **'ss'** or **'mit'** first.
- To add **'cian'** take off the **'s'** or **'cs'** first.

1. **Add the correct ending – 'tion', 'sion', 'ssion' or 'cian' – to the words
   in the assembly line using the rules above. Remember that when
   words end in 'e', you take the 'e' off before adding the prefix.**

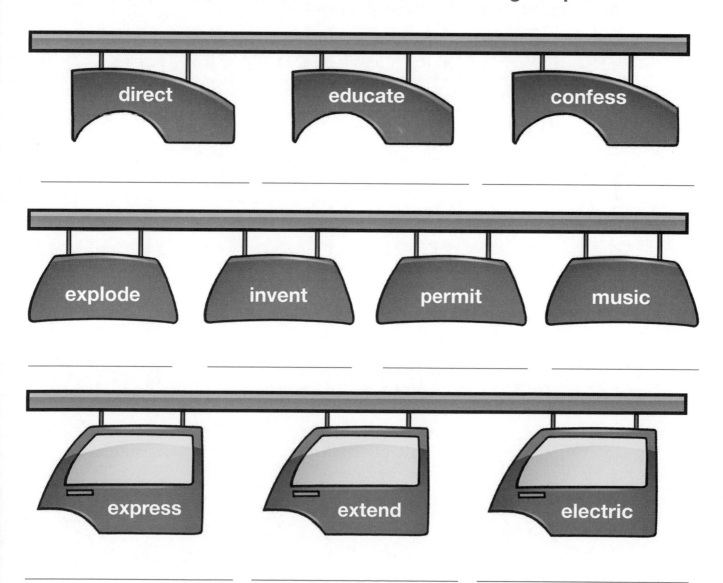

direct   educate   confess

explode   invent   permit   music

express   extend   electric

A chorus line

The letters **'ch'** make three different sounds. **/ch/** – *chocolate*, **/sh/** – *machine* and **/k/ –** *echo*. The **/sh/** sound is usually found in French words that we use: *chef*.

1. **Choose three coloured pens and use them to highlight the /ch/ sound words, /sh/ sound words and /k/ sound words.**

> chorus   chair   brochure   chemist   technical   much
> chute   branch   quiche   crochet   church   ricochet   monarch
> architect   orchid   ache   chandelier   chivalry   cheek

2. **Now sort the words into these boxes.**

/k/	/sh/	/ch/

'gue' and 'que'

Words that have the endings **'gue'** and **'que'** mostly originate from French words. In French, the letter **'q'** is pronounced **/k/**.

'gue' sound like **/g/**: *plague*   **'que'** sounds like **/k/**: *plaque*

1. **Complete the words below with either 'gue' or 'que'. Write the finished words into the correct buildings.**

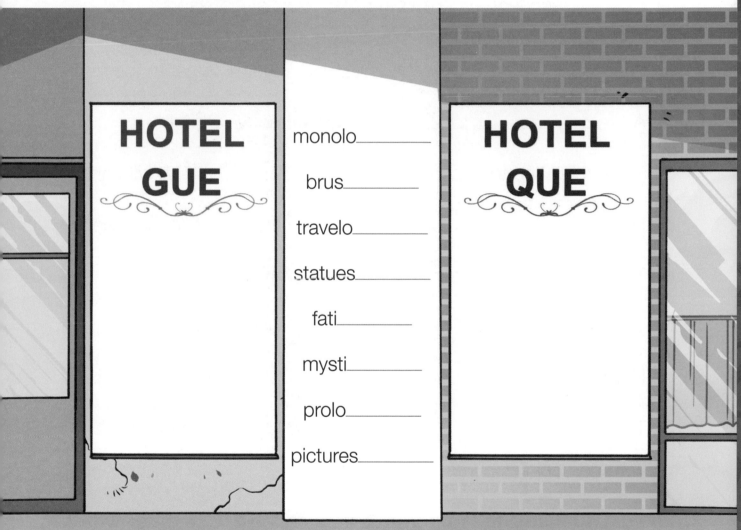

HOTEL
GUE

monolo_____

brus_____

travelo_____

statues_____

fati_____

mysti_____

prolo_____

pictures_____

HOTEL
QUE

2. **Choose one 'gue' word and one 'que' word from question 1. Write them in sentences of your own.**

_____

_____

_____

The science of 'sc'

In some words the **/s/** is made by **'sc'**. These words come from older Latin words and in Roman times **'c'** was probably pronounced as **'s'**.

1. Complete the sentences with the 'sc' words from the box.

> ascend   crescent   descend   fascinated   scene
> scenery   scent   science   scientist   scissors

a. I began to _____ the hill to get to the top.

b. A _____ moon is not very bright.

c. The farmer had to _____ the hill with his sheep.

d. I was _____ with the picture in the gallery.

e. The _____ was very beautiful.

f. The _____ of the perfume was quite strong.

g. I had to use the _____ to cut the string.

h. The _____ discovered a cure for the

common cold.

2. You did not use two of the words in question 1. Use these words in sentences of your own.

_____

_____

_____

_____

Correct the spelling

The sound **/ai/** can be spelled in lots of different ways: **'a–e'**, **'ai'**, **'ay'**, **'ei'**, **'eigh'** and **'ey'**! There is no rule, they just have to be learned.

1. These words are not spelled correctly. Write the correct spellings using the meanings to help you.

whay   _____   You separate this to make cheese.

nai   _____   The sound a horse makes.

slaigh   _____   Transport for snowy weather.

rayn   _____   Horses have these.

convai   _____   To tell or pass on information.

wai   _____   To measure how heavy something is.

prai   _____   You can go to a place of worship to do this.

preigh   _____   An animal that is being hunted.

vail   _____   A bride might wear one.

Spelling

A dear heard

1. **Read the passage below. Circle the incorrect homophones and write the correct versions above.**

I once went walking through a park. It was a beautiful day and I saw a

heard of dear. They sat in the shade of a huge oak tree. The hole heard

was peacefully chewing grass as I walked by. Suddenly, I herd a shout and

a man was chasing towards the deer. He ran so fast that he didn't see a

whole in the ground, he tripped and fell in. Oh deer I thought as he didn't

look very happy climbing back out of the whole.

2. **Now complete the table with the pairs of words you have found.**

Word	Meaning
heard	listened to

Creating nouns (1)

Prefixes are a group of letters that go in front of a word and change the meaning of the word.

- **'hyper'** means *over, beyond, above.*
- **'kilo'** means one *thousand.*
- **'mega'** means *large.*

1. **Match each word below with the 'mega', 'kilo' or 'hyper' prefix to create a new noun. Write the new word in the correct elephant.**

market   metre   link   active   byte   gram   star   city

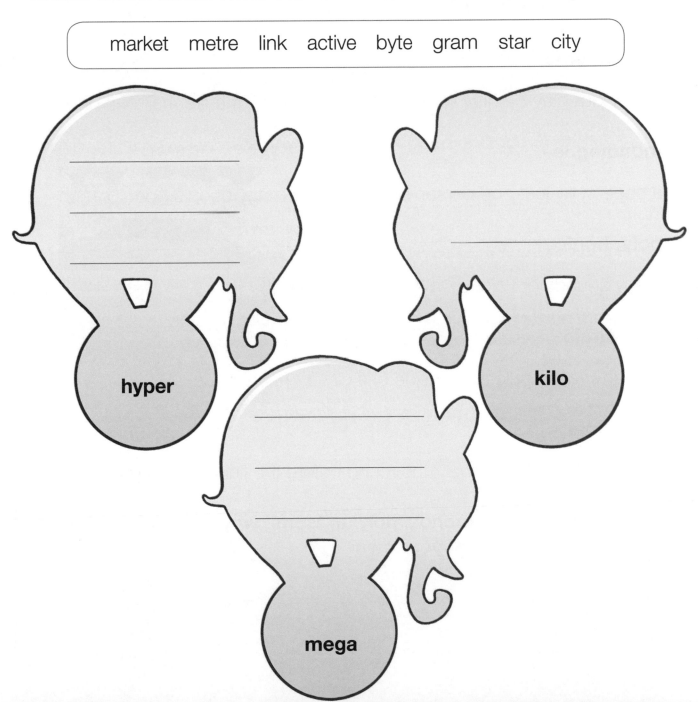

hyper

kilo

mega

Creating nouns (2)

1. **Find out the meaning of the following prefixes.**

   mono _____

   poly _____

   semi _____

2. **Use your knowledge to circle the correct meaning for these 'mono', 'poly' and 'semi' words.**

   monodrama

   a very dull play / a play with just one performer / the first half of a play

   monologue

   a speech by just one person / a speech for many people / one branch

   polyphonic

   many sounds or voices / a musical instrument

   semicircle

   a quarter of a circle / the inside of a circle / half a circle

   semi-final

   half way through the final / the round before the final / a little final

3. **Choose one of the 'mono', 'poly' or 'semi' words from question 2. Use it in a sentence of your own.**

   _____

   _____

From *aqua* to *aquarium*

Many word families use a **root** from an older language, such as Latin. Knowing the root word and its meaning can help you to increase your vocabulary, and also help you to spell other words from the same family.

1. All of the words below use roots from an older language. Read the root word and then the modern word. Find more modern words that belong to that word family.

Root word	Modern word	More words
aqua (water)	aquarium	_____ _____
audio (hear)	audience	_____ _____
centum (hundred)	century	_____ _____
liber (free)	liberty	_____ _____
navis (ship)	navy	_____ _____
plus (more)	surplus	_____ _____

Provide a pronoun

1. **Improve the sentences below by replacing a *noun* with a *pronoun* when the noun has been repeated.**

   a. Amra fell heavily. Amra hurt her knee.

   _____

   b. I have a cat. I am very fond of that cat.

   _____

   c. The magnet belongs to Tom. The magnet is very powerful.

   _____

   _____

   d. Debbie and I went to the library to get a book. Debbie and I found the book.

   _____

   _____

   e. James is a tall boy. James is very athletic. I admire James.

   _____

   _____

   f. Jane was very careless. Jane lost her purse. Luckily, on her way home, Jane found her purse.

   _____

   _____

Being clear

Using lots of pronouns can make who is doing the actions unclear.

Jack and his friend went to the library. He gave him a book to read.

Who gave who the book? Was it the boy or the friend?

Jack and his friend went to the library. Jack gave his friend a book to read.

It is now clear who gave who the book.

1. **Change some, or all, of the pronouns in these sentences to make them easier to understand.**

   a. Bill went to the park and met John. He gave him a football.

   _____

   _____

   b. In the middle of the field, the girl saw her mum. She beckoned her to come to her.

   _____

   _____

   c. He looked through the window and saw his uncle. He waved at him.

   _____

   _____

   d. He tripped and fell on the ice and pulled over his friend. He helped him up.

   _____

   _____

Grammar

Expressing time, place and cause

Conjunctions, prepositions and adverbs can express time, place and cause within a sentence and between sentences.

- Time is when something happens: *next, during, immediately.*
- Cause is why something happened: *because.*
- Place is where something happened: *inside.*

1. **Read the passage below and circle any words that express time, place or cause.**

I went to my friend's house because we were doing our homework together.

We worked until it was lunchtime. I went back home after I visited the

library. Since I hadn't finished my homework, I decided to finish it after tea.

I watched some television then Mum said it was teatime. We had sausage

and mash and afterwards we had ice cream. The dog was sitting beside the

table waiting for scraps. My brother went back to watch television while I

had to finish my homework.

2. **Complete the sentences below with words that express time, place or cause.**

   a. I went to bed _____ I was tired.

   b. We went to the café for lunch _____ we went to the cinema.

   c. I have lived in this house _____ the day I was born.

   d. The boy didn't hand in his homework _____ he got told off.

e. It was left on the floor _____ the rubbish bin.

f. _____ it will be my birthday.

g. I will do my work _____ I will watch some television.

h. I found the key _____ the mess in the drawer

i. I will wait here _____ your train leaves.

j. _____ the performance, the man ate crisps noisily.

3. Complete the Time Lord's instructions using your choice of time, place and cause words.

To retrieve my Sonic Abacus please follow these simple

instructions. _____ go quickly downstairs and look

_____ the table for a banana _____ I'm

a bit peckish _____ I've been too busy for breakfast.

_____ we will need the Byzantium Key which your mum is

currently using as a hoover. I left it here _____ my previous

visit and the disguise has worked perfectly! _____ you

have secured the Key I can unlock the Aztec Portal and we'll all be home

_____ elevenses.

Determiners

Sometimes a noun is an item that is well-known to us, for example *my* dog, *that* dog over there.

Sometimes a noun is an item that we don't know well, for example *a* dog, *some* dogs.

All of the words in bold above are called *determiners*. They specify how well we know a noun and can tell us how many, whose and which.

Determiners

the   a   an   three   six
many   some   both   first   this
that   many

Nouns

flower   dog   boy   crocodile
door   stairs   school   children
trees   river   stars   cup

1. **Choose six determiners and six nouns from the chart above. Use them to make up six sentences.**

_____

_____

_____

_____

_____

_____

_____

_____

Expanded noun phrases

Expanded noun phrases give us more information. They can contain adjectives and preposition phrases, as well as the noun.

The girl with the big smile *spoke to her friends.*

1. Underline the expanded noun phrases in the sentences below.

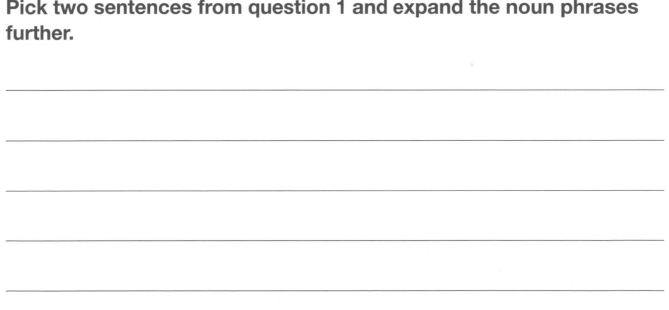

a. I think it was those boys over there!

b. The big black clouds moved overhead.

c. I really I like the lesson after maths.

d. This garden overgrown with weeds was a secret.

e. The fast red car went speeding down the road.

f. I saw the silly little kittens in the basket.

g. You can add the extra words before the noun and after it.

h. The big black clouds, with a menacing rumble, moved overhead.

2. Pick two sentences from question 1 and expand the noun phrases further.

_____

_____

_____

_____

Adverbials

Sometimes, we use more than one word to provide more information about a verb. This is called an **adverbial**.

*The bus leaves **in five minutes**.*

in five minutes tells us when the bus will leave.

An adverbial usually answers questions such as *How?*, *When/How long for?* and *Where?*

1. **Look at the sentences below. Underline the adverbials.**

   a. Jill shut the door quietly.

   b. I promised to meet Bob outside the shop.

   c. The bath, like a bubbly haven, was Sally's ultimate goal of the day.

   d. I will start my homework in a couple of minutes.

   e. I tripped over the bag when I got off the bus.

   f. We met when we started school.

   g. I got to see my favourite band after hours of queuing.

   h. There were chocolates, sweets, biscuits and cakes left by the kind lady.

2. **What do you notice about where the adverbial comes in the sentence?**

   _____

   _____

   _____

   _____

Matching adverbials

Adverbials do not always have to come at the end of a sentence.
Sometimes they come at the beginning. When they do, we use a comma after them.

*I'm visiting my grandma **at the weekend**.*

***At the weekend**, I am visiting my grandma.*

1. **Add the adverbial to each sentence. First write the adverbial at the end. Then write the sentence again with the adverbial at the beginning – remember the comma!**

I will tidy my room.   **Adverbial:** before I do my homework

_____

_____

_____

It will be the holidays.   **Adverbial:** after tomorrow

_____

_____

_____

I tiptoed into the room.   **Adverbial:** slowly and stealthily

_____

_____

_____

Writing fronted adverbials

1. Use these adverbials to write sentences of your own. Only use the adverbials at the beginning of the sentences.

> fast and furiously   before we go   when I got off the bus in a flash
> after tomorrow   slowly and quietly   impatiently and grumpily
> at the end of the week

_____

_____

_____

_____

_____

_____

_____

_____

_____

_____

_____

_____

We was or we were?

Standard English can be spoken or written. It is the form that is usually used in formal writing and it can be used in all accents. It is seen as the 'correct' form.

Non-standard English is usually used in speech and can vary in different places. You would not usually use this for writing.

For example:

- **Standard English:** *I did* my homework.
- **Non-standard English:** *I done* my homework.

1. **Tick each sentence to say whether it is standard English or non-standard English.**

	Non-standard	Standard
I did not see the chair and fell over it.		
Yes, I've seen them books.		
We was playing at home in my garden.		
I ain't felling very well.		
I was happy about winning the race.		
Me mum says I have to go now.		

2. **Choose two of the non-standard sentences from question 1. Rewrite them in standard English.**

_____

_____

The apostrophe

Apostrophes can be used to show that a letter is missing:

she is – she's

Apostrophes are also used to show that something belongs to someone or something:

Shane's cup

1. Correct the sentences below by inserting the apostrophes.

I didnt want to ask, but I had to find out if they were Joes socks.

There wasnt any food in the cupboard so I took Mums chocolate.

The flowerpot was knocked over by Katies dog.

I hadnt seen the boy run away, but my friends had.

I wasnt going to see my sisters concert.

Somehow I wasnt going to let my brothers prank upset me.

In the end it didnt go according to plan.

Bens football team was winning, but he wasnt there to watch.

Plural or possessive?

To make a noun plural you add **'s'**: *jacket**s***

To show that something or someone belongs to a noun you add an apostrophe then an **'s'**: *Jane**'s** jackets*

If the noun is a plural and already ends in **'s'**, add the apostrophe on the end: *the girl**s'** jackets*

1. **Read these sentences and circle the mistakes. Then rewrite the words correctly.**

There are several birds' in the gardens. _____

The birds nests are in the tree. _____

Ellie Jennings has several pen's in her

pencil case. _____

At St Winifred's, the girls swimming team

and hockey team are fierce rivals. _____

In the shop I saw shoes', trouser, top's and

jumper, but I did not like any of them. _____

Alex kicked the dogs ball over the fence. _____

The girls' are going to find the boys hideout. _____

There are no cakes' in the shop as they

have all been eaten. _____

Comma time

A comma is used in sentences to separate lists.

1. **Rewrite these sentences, adding in the commas in the correct place.**

I went swimming and had to bring my costume towel goggles and float.

_____

_____

Leila's dress was an astonishing mix of pink blue red and yellow.

_____

_____

I like eating apples bananas, grapes and pickles.

_____

_____

To get to my friend's house you have to turn left then right and go straight on.

_____

_____

I'd like to play on the slide the climbing frame the swings and the zip wire.

_____

_____

In the field I saw a poppy a cornflower and a butterfly.

_____

At the beginning

An **adverbial** is a group of words that modifies a verb. When we use these at the beginning of a sentence, we put a comma after it.

1. **Add the missing comma after the adverbials in these sentences.**

After school I went to my swimming lessons.

While I was at the party my mum took my brother to the shops.

In the morning I will get up and walk the dog.

After the pantomime we went to have ice cream in the café.

During the race I tripped up and fell down.

Later that day he found his book and his pen.

The day after tomorrow I will be going on holiday.

Before we start I need to tell you the rules.

Punctuating direct speech

In direct speech, related punctuation goes inside the speech marks.
One sentence: comma before the tag word inside speech marks.
Speech marks at beginning and end of direct words spoken.

"I can't go out in this weather or I shall get soaked to the skin," said Mo.

Two sentences: comma before tag word inside speech marks.
Full stop after speaker's name. End full stop inside speech marks.
Speech marks close and re-open either side of tag-word and speaker.

"I can't go out in this weather," said Mo. *"I shall get soaked to the skin."*

One sentence, broken in the middle by tag word and speaker's name.
Comma before first close of speech marks, comma after tag word or name,
lower-case letter to continue the sentence after the tag word. Full stop inside
the speech marks at the end.

"I can't go out in this weather," Mo said, *"or I shall get soaked to the skin,
won't I?"*

1. Punctuate the following sentences.

a. In the winter the weather gets cold but snow usually falls
only on the hills explained Mr Smith

b. In the summer it is warmer Mr Smith added so the sheep
will graze on higher ground

c. In the autumn and spring the weather varies he continued
Sheep can be found on high and low ground

d. I am never sure whether I prefer winter or summer said
Adam but I do like building snowmen

Presenting dialogue

1. **Read the dialogue between Lucy and her dog Sam. Rewrite it as a passage of text, adding detail about how each speech is spoken. Remember to start a new line for each new speaker and to use the correct punctuation for speech.**

Listen, Sam, that must be the newspaper boy!

Lucy

Woof! Woof!

dog

I wonder if you can remember what you learned at dog school? Take the paper to dad. Now fetch!

Lucy

Oh, Sam.

Lucy's dad

Did it work?

Lucy

Sort of. He fetched the paper but it's all torn.

Lucy's dad

_____

_____

_____

_____

_____

Lost wallet

In the passage below, two boys face a dilemma.

The bus slowed down and stopped. It was the stop before school. One man got off, but Balraj and Ben hardly noticed him, until they realised that he had left something behind – a wallet. Balraj picked it up and shouted after the man, but it was too late. The bus had already started again.

He sat back down and Ben said, "Here, let's have a look." Balraj passed over the wallet, and Ben opened it. "Hey, there's a five-pound note here!" he said.

"You're not thinking of keeping it?" said Balraj.

"Why not?" said Ben. "Finders keepers."

"It's not worth being dishonest just for five pounds," said Balraj. "You could earn that quickly just by mowing Granny Smith's lawn!"

"What if it were £1000?" said Ben.

"Er..." Balraj hesitated, "well, I suppose it's still the same! You'd better give that wallet to me and I'll hand it in."

Balraj took the wallet and looked through it. "Look, here's his address," he said after a moment, "and...what's this?"

He took out a folded piece of paper. He unfolded it and spread it out between them. It was a roughly sketched map. The main city on the map was Porto Paso in South America and there was a dotted line to a place marked with compass bearings. Somebody had scribbled near the bearings: 'Inca gold here.'

"It's a treasure map!" exclaimed Ben. "That settles it. We keep the wallet and the map and go and find the treasure. We'll be rich!"

"Find the treasure – what with?" said Balraj. "Do you know how much a ticket to South America will cost?"

"I'll save up for it!"

"Yeah, for about ten years! I think this map makes it even more important to give the wallet back."

Read the passage on page 44 and answer the questions below.

1. **What is the dilemma?**

   _____

2. **What do you think the boys should do if this was a real-life incident?**

   _____

3. **What do you think will happen in the story?**

   _____

4. **What stories have you read that have the theme of a dilemma?**

   _____

5. **Here are some dilemmas. Pick one and write two alternate outcomes for it.**

   Jenna has promised her mum that she will revise properly for an exam next week. But she has been invited to the cinema tomorrow afternoon.

   Jonathan is ten steps away from the golden statue. But the door to the treasure chamber is closing right NOW.

   Princess Genevieve knows she can outsmart the troll and get back to the castle in time for dinner. But Sir Gifford is trying very hard to impress her.

   _____

   _____

   _____

   _____

Heraldry

1. **Read the following passage and underline the key facts.**

When a medieval knight was in full armour his face was covered with a helmet so it was impossible to decide who he was or even for whom he was fighting! In order for his supporters to recognise him, the knight would wear a 'coat of arms' over his armour. This led to the practice of putting the same designs on the shield.

A shield was divided into nine main areas. Across the top of the shield were the 'dexter chief', the 'centre chief' and the 'sinister chief'. Below these were the 'dexter flank', the 'fess point' (the centre of the shield) and the 'sinister flank'. The bottom third of the shield was divided into 'dexter base', the 'centre base' and the 'sinister base'.

In Latin, 'dexter' means right and 'sinister' means left, but a shield was always decorated as seen from the point of view of the knight *behind* the shield.

Only certain colours were used to paint the shield – red, blue, black, green and purple – and only two metals could be used – silver and gold. The knights also chose to divide the shield with horizontal, vertical or chevron lines. Finally they added drawings of things such as griffins, eagles, rampant lions, trees, flowers and weapons. When one rich family married another their shield emblems were often combined and became more complicated.

Glossary

chevron a V shape

griffin an animal that is part eagle, part lion

rampant standing on its back legs

coat of arms a decorated tunic

---

2. **Use the key facts you found to summarise the text in one paragraph.**

_____

_____

_____

_____

_____

_____

_____

3. **Now decorate the shield following the instructions below and using the information given in the passage.**

- three horizontal lines in dexter chief
- a sun in fess point
- three vertical lines in sinister chief
- five horizontal lines which cover dexter base and centre base
- two chevrons in the dexter flank
- a rampant lion which covers sinister flank and sinister base
- a bird in the centre chief
- Colour your shield in suitable colours.

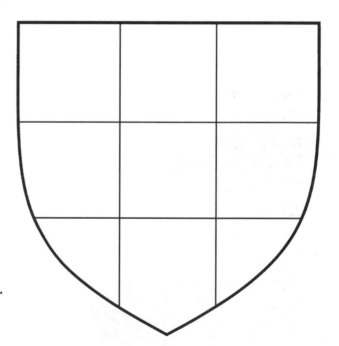

! Don't forget left is right as you look at the shield.

Cats

Cats sleep

Anywhere,

Any table,

Any chair,

Top of piano,

Window-ledge,

In the middle,

On the edge,

Open drawer,

Empty shoe,

Anybody's

Lap will do,

Fitted in a

Cardboard box,

In the cupboard

With your frocks –

Anywhere!

They don't care!

Cats sleep

Anywhere.

Eleanor Farjeon

Poets often use **rhyming words** at the end of poem lines. This helps to give a poem interesting sound effects.

Read the poem on page 48 and answer the questions.

1. Write pairs of rhyming words from the poem 'Cats'.

   anywhere   chair _____   _____

   _____   _____

Adjectives give extra details about nouns. They help to make the language of poetry rich and atmospheric.

2. Write down three adjectives from the poem 'Cats'.

   _____   _____

   _____

3. What words are repeated in 'Cats'?

   _____

   What effect does this repetition give?

   _____

4. Draw a box around your favourite section of the poem. Explain why you like it.

   _____

   _____

Water cycle

The Earth's water is 97 per cent salt water and 3 per cent fresh water. Of the fresh water, 17 per cent is free-flowing and 83 per cent is frozen. So only a tiny part of Earth's water is for people, plants and animals to share. Since the amount of water is constant, we must use the fresh water over and over again.

Different states

Water is the only substance to exist naturally as three states of matter. Water is found as a solid when it freezes to form ice. It freezes at 0 °C. Above 0 °C, it melts to form liquid water. When liquid water is heated, it evaporates and turns into a gas called water vapour. Water can evaporate at almost any temperature above freezing. For example, the water in wet washing will evaporate even on a cool day.

How clouds form

Water evaporates from the surface of rivers, lakes, seas and oceans, and from the leaves of plants. As water vapour rises, it cools. It condenses back to form tiny droplets of water. Millions of these droplets form rain clouds. With more moisture, the droplets get bigger and then fall to the ground.

An endless cycle

Water droplets that fall from clouds are called precipitation. Some precipitation is soaked up by the ground and plants. Some drains into rivers, lakes, seas and oceans, where it evaporates and the whole process begins again. This is called the water cycle.

Read the text on page 50 and then answer the questions below.

1. **What kind of text is this?**

   Instruction ☐

   Report ☐

   Explanation ☐

2. **What are the features of this text, for example headings, subheadings?**

   _____

   _____

3. **Find and write any words expressing cause.**

   _____

   _____

4. **Summarise the text in five sentences.**

   _____

   _____

   _____

   _____

   _____

Composition

Paragraphs

Paragraphs help to structure your writing, making it easier to read. Paragraphs are used to group information and are organised around a theme.

1. **Read the following text and then write what you think is the main theme of each paragraph.**

In South America there is a tall mountain range called the Andes. The air is thin and cold there and so people have to keep warm by wearing thick woollen capes called ponchos.	*Introduces the story and the setting, for example what it is like in the mountains.*
On one of the mountains is a farm. It belongs to the family of a small boy called Pedro. Pedro's family don't live at the farm. They have a house in the city but visit their farm once a year.	_____ _____
One cold day Pedro's father took him to visit their farm. They rode on horseback up the mountain.	_____
The farm dogs started barking. One dog was small and friendly. When Pedro called to it, the dog wagged its tail. When he jumped down from his horse the dog licked Pedro's hand, "It looks like you've made a friend!" laughed Pedro's father.	_____ _____ _____
Later that day, Pedro's father decided they should set off home. They mounted their horses and set off down the mountain. The dog, quietly followed his new friend all the way home!	_____ _____

Flying machines

In non-fiction writing, paragraphs are sometimes introduced by **subheadings**.

1. **Read the passage about flying machines and pick out four separate paragraphs grouping related material. Mark the beginning of each paragraph with the symbol //.**

For centuries man has dreamed of being able to fly. As long ago as the 15th century, Leonardo da Vinci drew sketches of flying machines. However, he was ahead of his time and his machines were impossible to build with the tools of the day. Man's first successful flight took place in 1783. The Montgolfier brothers filled a large paper balloon with hot smoke from a fire, and it floated 1800 metres into the air. To the people watching, it seemed a miracle, but balloons and airships soon became common. The first flight by an aeroplane took place in 1903, at Kitty Hawk, in the USA. The aeroplane had been made by two brothers, Orville and Wilbur Wright. Though gliders had been flown successfully for many years, the importance of this invention was that it allowed for long-distance flight. The most exciting flight of all must be the journey to the moon. On 20 July,1969, United States astronauts Neil Armstrong and Edwin Aldrin took off in one of the mighty Apollo rockets and travelled to the moon. They landed in the Sea of Tranquillity. They did several experiments, and then took off for Earth with soil and rock samples. After a trouble-free flight, they landed safely.

2. **Think of a suitable subheading for each paragraph you identified. Write them below.**

1. _____   3. _____

2. _____   4. _____

Life cycle of a flowering plant

Use the illustrations to write paragraphs on the life cycle of a plant. Each picture will help to group information about each step in the life cycle.

Into the picture

1. What are these people thinking? What are they saying? Where have they come from? Where are they going? Write some of your ideas in the boxes.

African elephants

1. **Use the fact card to write a report about elephants. Choose an appropriate heading and then use the words in bold as subheadings.**

Remember to include:
- an introductory sentence
- technical/specific vocabulary
- factual descriptions.

African elephant

Appearance large four-legged animals, grey in colour, long trunk), tusks, large rounded ears

Habitat savannah landscape in Africa, elephants live in herds

Food leaves, branches, grasses, bark, fruit

Average life span 70 years

Size height 2.5m to 4m

Alien planet and other settings

Planning the **settings** of your story is important.

When you plan your settings ask yourself the question: What can your character see, smell or hear? This will start to create the picture of the settings. Think about the weather. A story set in the mountains might have snowy weather, whereas a story set at the beach might have sunny weather.

Alien planet

Theme park

Factory

1. **Choose one of the pictures above as a setting for a story. Look at the scene carefully, then develop it in note form by:**

- thinking of adjectives and figures of speech to describe it
- drawing a map of the area and adding place names and other details, especially those which could be used in a story, such as a deep well.

Planet in danger story

The **plot** describes the main events in the story, the problems your character faces and how they are resolved through the introduction, build up, conflict, climax and resolution.

1. **List the possible side effects of each of these planetary problems. Try to suggest one way in which each problem could be solved.**

Food starts to run out

Effects _____

Solution _____

A strange disease breaks out

Effects _____

Solution _____

Poisonous fumes start to poison the air

Effects _____

Solution _____

Attack by another planet

Effects _____

Solution _____

2. Use the story mountain to plan a story about a problem faced by beings on a planet. Remember to include progression in your plot for the story's beginning, middle and end.

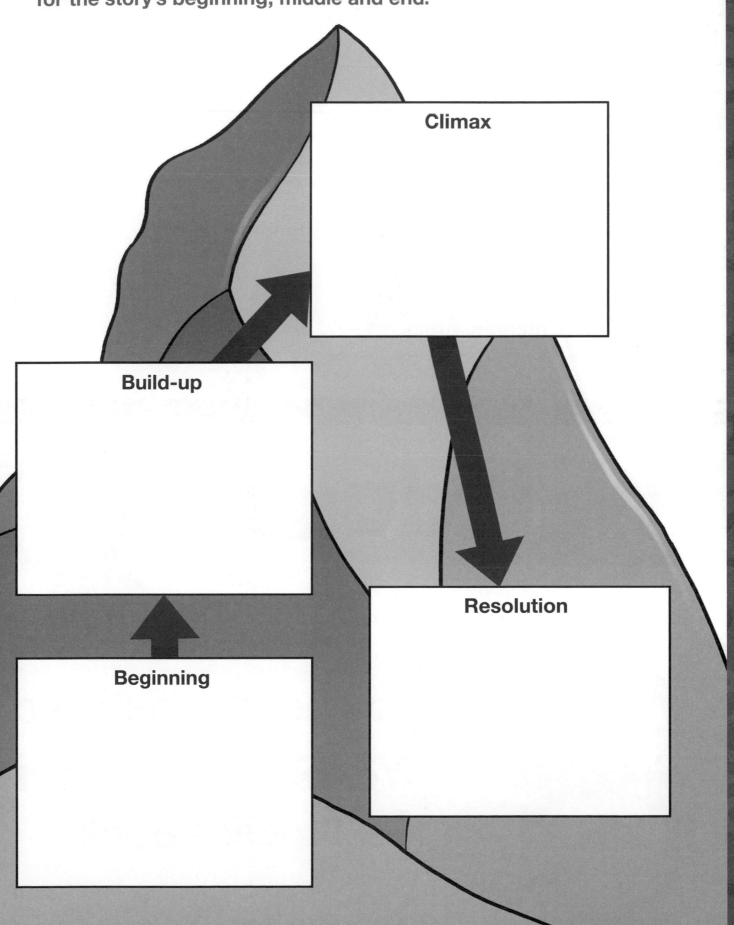

Climax

Build-up

Resolution

Beginning

Progress chart

Making progress? Tick (✔) the flower boxes as you complete each section of the book.

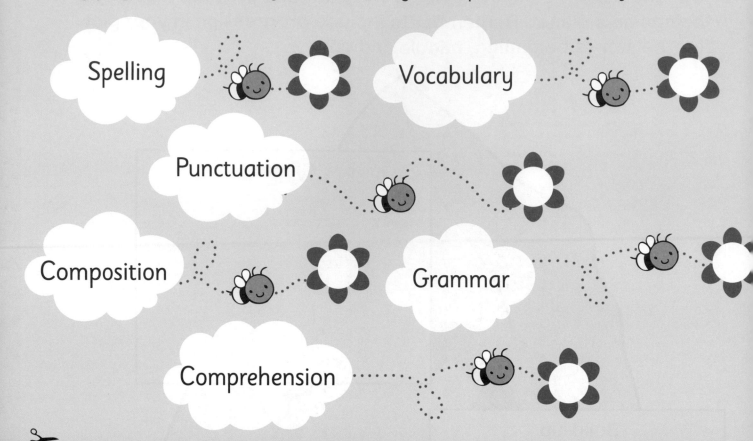

Spelling

Vocabulary

Punctuation

Composition

Grammar

Comprehension

Well done!

YOU DID IT! ★

Name: _____

You have completed
YEAR 4 ENGLISH
Practice Book

Age: _____   Date: _____

Answers

The answers are given below. They are referenced by page number and where applicable, question number. The answers usually only include the information the children are expected to give.

Note that answers in literacy will be varied and subjective from child to child, and a fair degree of marker discretion and interpretation is needed, particularly if children's understanding and skills have to be deduced from their answers.

Page number	Question number	Answers
6	1	peeler, marvellous, perilous, controllable/controller, novelist, finalist, traveller, propeller, signaller, jeweller, footballer
7	1	hysterical, symptom, lyrics, symmetry, sympathy, crystal, system, mystery, typical, cygnet
8	1a	touch
	1b	young
	1c	country
	1d	couple
	1e	double
	1f	cousin
	1g	flourish
	1h	tough
	1i	encourage
9	1	For this style of question, refer to a dictionary for the answers.
	2a	illegal – Children's own sentence.
	2b	illogical – Children's own sentence.
	2c	irregular – Children's own sentence.
	2d	irresistible – Children's own sentence.
	2e	irreversible – Children's own sentence.
	2f	irrational – Children's own sentence.
10	1	inaudible, inconvenient, incorrect, inhuman, immobile, immortal, impolite, impossible, insane, invisible
11	1	**re:** refresh, reappear, redecorate, retreat, rearrange **inter:** interlude, interrelated, intercontinental, interface, intermingle
12	1	subcategory, substandard, supercomputer, subeditor, subsonic/supersonic, superimpose, submerge, superpower
	2	Children's own answers.
13	1	admiration, relocation, justification, translation, animation, education, observation, accommodation, anticipation, identification
14	1	angrily, anxiously, badly, carefully, clumsily, correctly, greedily, happily, hungrily, immediately, quietly, seriously
15	1	incredibly, hostilely, probably, agilely, terribly
	2	probably, incredibly, agilely, hostilely, terribly
16	1	**zh:** measure, pleasure, pressure, composure, exposure, leisure **sh:** ensure, reassure, unsure
17	1	adventure, agriculture, architecture, furniture, future, mixture, structure, miniature, creature, texture

Page number	Question number	Answers
18	1	courageous, harmonious, envious, poisonous, glorious, famous, various, adventurous, luxurious, outrageous
19	1	direction, education, confession, explosion, invention, permission, musician, expression, extension, electrician
20	1	**ch**orus, **ch**air, bro**ch**ure, **ch**emist, te**ch**nical, mu**ch**, **ch**ute, bran**ch**, qui**che**, cro**ch**et, **ch**ur**ch**, rico**ch**et, monar**ch**, ar**ch**itect, or**ch**id, a**che**, **ch**andelier, **ch**ivalry, **ch**eek
	2	**/k/:** chorus, chemist, technical, monarch, architect, orchid, ache **/sh/:** brochure, chute, quiche, crochet, ricochet, chandelier, chivalry **/ch/:** chair, much, branch, church, cheek
21	1	**Hotel Gue:** fatigue, monologue, prologue, travelogue **Hotel Que:** brusque, mystique, picturesque, statuesque
	2	Children's own answers.
22	1	ascend, crescent, descend, fascinated, scenery, scent, scissors, scientist
	2	Children's own answers for 'science' and 'scene'.
23	1	whey, neigh, sleigh, rein, convey, weigh, pray, prey, veil
24	1	heard – herd, dear – deer, hole – whole, heard – herd, herd – heard, whole – hole, deer – dear, whole – hole
	2	For this style of question, refer to a dictionary for the answers.
25	1	**Hyper:** hypermarket, hyperlink, hyperactive **Kilo:** kilometre, kilogram **Mega:** megabyte, megastar, megacity
	2	Children's own answers.
26	1	mono – one, poly – many, semi – half
	2	monodrama – a play with just one performer. monologue – a speech by just one person. polyphonic – many sounds and voices. semicircle – half a circle. semi-final – the round before the final.
	3	Children's own answers.
27	1	Children's own answers.
28	1a	Amra fell heavily. She hurt her knee.
	1b	I have a cat. I am very fond of it.
	1c	The magnet belongs to Tom. It is very powerful.
	1d	Debbie and I went to the library to get a book. We found the book.
	1e	James is a tall boy. He is very athletic. I admire him.
	1f	Jane was very careless. She lost her purse. Luckily, on her way home, she found it.
29	1	Children's own answers.
30	1	The following words should be circled: because, until, after, since, after, then, afterwards, beside, while
	2a	Children's own answers.
	2b	Children's own answers.
	2c	Children's own answers.
	2d	Children's own answers.

Page number	Question number	Answers
31	2e	Children's own answers.
	2f	Children's own answers.
	2g	Children's own answers.
	2h	Children's own answers.
	2i	Children's own answers.
	2j	Children's own answers.
	3	Children's own answers.
32	1	Children's own answers.
33	1a	those boys over there
	1b	the big black clouds
	1c	the lesson after maths
	1d	this garden overgrown with weeds
	1e	the fast red car
	1f	the silly little kittens in the basket
	1g	the extra words before the noun and after it
	1h	the big black clouds, with a menacing rumble
	2	Children's own answers.
34	1a	quietly
	1b	outside the shop
	1c	of the day
	1d	in a couple of minutes
	1e	when I got off the bus
	1f	when we started school
	1g	after hours of queuing
	1h	by the kind lady
	2	After the verb.
35	1	I will tidy my room before I do my homework. Before I do my homework, I will tidy my room. It will be the holidays after tomorrow. After tomorrow, it will be the holidays. I tiptoed into the room slowly and stealthily. Slowly and stealthily, I tiptoed into the room.
36	1	Children's own answers.

37 — 1

	Non-standard	Standard
I did not see the chair and fell over it.		✓
Yes, I've seen them books.	✓	
We was playing at home in my garden.	✓	
I ain't felling very well.	✓	
I was happy about winning the race.		✓
Me mum says I have to go now.	✓	

Page number	Question number	Answers
	2	Children's own answers.
38	1	didn't, Joe's, wasn't, Mum's, Katie's, hadn't, wasn't, sister's, wasn't, brother's, didn't, Ben's, wasn't
39	1	birds' – birds, birds – birds', pen's – pens, girls – girls', shoes' – shoes, trouser – trousers, top's – tops, jumper – jumpers, dogs – dog's, girls' – girls, boys – boys'/boy's, cakes' – cakes

Page number	Question number	Answers
40	1	I went swimming and had to bring my costume, towel, goggles and float. Leila's dress was an astonishing mix of pink, blue, red and yellow. I like eating apples, bananas, grapes and pickles. To get to my friend's house you have to turn left, then right and go straight on. I'd like to play on the slide, the climbing frame, the swings and the zip wire. In the field I saw a poppy, a cornflower and a butterfly.
41	1	After school, I went to my swimming lessons. While I was at the party, my mum took my brother to the shops. In the morning, I will get up and walk the dog. After the pantomime, we went to have ice cream in the café. During the race, I tripped up and fell down. Later that day, he found his book and his pen. The day after tomorrow, I will be going on holiday. Before we start, I need to tell you the rules.
42	1a	"In the winter, the weather gets cold but snow usually falls only on the hills," explained Mr Smith.
	1b	"In the summer, it is warmer," Mr Smith added, "so the sheep will graze on higher ground."
	1c	"In the autumn and spring, the weather varies," he continued. "Sheep can be found on high and low ground."
	1d	"I am never sure whether I prefer winter or summer," said Adam, "but I do like building snowmen."
43	1	Children's own answers.
45	1	Whether to return the money and wallet.
	2	Children's own answers.
	3	Children's own answers.
	4	Children's own answers.
	5	Children's own answers.
46	1	Children's own answers.
47	2	Children's own answers.
	3	Children's drawing.
49	1	anywhere – chair, ledge – edge, shoe – do, box – frocks, care – anywhere
	2	open, empty, cardboard
	3	cats, sleep, anywhere, any, the, in, a Creates regular rhythm.
	4	Children's own answers.
51	1	explanation
	2	explaining how something is happening and why, headings, subheadings, diagrams, present tense
	3	so, since, when, as, with
	4	Children's own answers.
52	1	Children's own answers.
53	1	Children's own answers.
	2	Children's own answers.
54		Children's own answers.
55	1	Children's own answers.
56	1	Children's own answers.
57	1	Children's own answers.
58	1	Children's own answers.
59	2	Children's own answers.